HANAUMA BAY
An Island Treasure

*This book
is dedicated
to those
who know
Secrets of
the Sea.*

Written By Liysa King
Photography By Don King

HANAUMA BAY

An Island Treasure was put together with visions of creating a greater appreciation of the ocean environment, as well as enhancing the reader's experiences at Hanauma. As more people become aware of the delicate and beautiful ecosystem in the sea, hopefully more significant measures will be enacted and enforced to protect it from pollution and destructive fishing practices, such as driftnetting.

The following individuals and organizations have been instrumental in the creation of this book: Bill McCorkle, biology instructor extraordinare; The Marine Option Program at the University of Hawai'i in Manoa which contributed a considerable amount of material to the book, both directly and indirectly; and the City and County lifeguards who shared stories and aloha, time and knowledge.

Others who assisted the project include: The Iaeas; Sam Ka'ai; XCEL Wetsuits; Alison Ledward; Bob Goodman; the Lipps; the De Witts; the Kings; the Smiths; Frank Parrish; John Jackson; Jim and Linda Howe; Mrs. F.E. Hines; Rob Phillips; Sherwood Maynard; the Mihos; Robyn Eric Thayer; Francis Haar; Art Reed; Mark Wildman and Danielle; Kawika; Mel (Shaka) Pu'u; Brian Keaulana; Walter Falconer; Kaeo Perez; Paul Turley; Pacific Stock; The Waikiki Aquarium; Sea Life Park; The Nature Conservancy; Bishop Museum and The Kamehameha Schools. To these and many others, I want to express my appreciation and aloha.

Mahalo Nui Loa.
Liysa King,
1990

MAHALO a'e ana au	I am appreciating
I ka nani a o Hanauma	The beauty of Hanauma
Ke kai ku'ono hala`i	The calm bay
Po'ai 'ia e na pali	encircled by cliffs
'Ua makemake nui 'ia	Greatly liked is
Ke alanui kike 'eke'e	the winding road
Eiho aku i lalo	that leads down
I ke kana one akea	To the broad sandy beach
He kahua na ka lehulehu	A place for the multitude
E luana hau'oli ai	To relax happily
E ho'olohe like a'e ana	Listening together
I ka leo o ke kai	To the soft voice of the sea
'Olu'olu ika pe'ahi	Cooled by the gentle fanning
A ka makani aheahe	Of the soft breeze
E ho'oluli malie ana	Gently swaying
I na lau o ke kiawe	The leaves of the kiawe
Ha'ina mai ka puana	This is the end of my story
No ka nani a o Hanauma	Of the beauty of Hanauma
Ke kai ku'ono hala'i	The calm bay
Po'ai 'ia e na pali	Encircled by cliffs.

This chant was written by Mary Kawena Pukui,
a beloved kupuna and rich resource of and for the people of Hawaii,
after she visited the bay many, many years ago...

Today, Hanauma is still enjoyed by the multitudes who relax happily together, sharing the enchantment and the excitement of discovery

It's a magically tangent space

Where the meeting of worlds takes place

With snorkels, masks, and fins, a kaleidoscopic world opens

*The powers of the sea are manifest in Hanauma's extremes—
an enveloping peace of white-light energy
and the overwhelming force of white-water energy*

Hanauma

is situated directly behind what was once the largest fishpond in the world. The dry climate of the bay was not practical for permanent residence, so it was used on a temporary basis by ancient Hawaiians.

Hawaiians have been coming to Hanauma for over 1000 years. Fishhooks dating back that far have been found in caves, and petroglyphs etched into the stone give evidence of long-standing use of the bay, which was part of the Maunalua ahupua'a (a form of land use division).

Kamehameha School brings students to Hanauma to study the environment and history. Here a class learns the art of uma wrestling.

The word *Hanauma* has several meanings in Hawaiian. *Hana*, in Hawaiian place names means *bay*, so technically, the term *"Hanauma Bay"* is redundant, but that's the popular name. *Uma* has three meanings, all of which can be applied to the place. *Uma* means *curved*, and can describe the curved beach. *Uma* was a form of wrestling, and Hanauma, besides being a favored fishing ground of kings and nobility, was a special place for hula competitions, festivals and wrestling contests. *Uma* is also the landing part of a canoe, and Hanauma's sheltered waters were used to harbor canoes until conditions were right for launching. It was also the most common landing point from Moloka'i crossings, due to the ocean currents.

In fact, Hawaiian legend has it that when Kanaloa and Kane, two of the four principal Hawaiian gods, came to O'ahu, they landed at Hanauma.

Moloka'i floats on the horizon across the Ka'iwi channel.

Hawaiian canoe paddlers and the uma of the canoe.

Iolani Luahine, a kumu hula of the hula kahiko (ancient hula) dancing at Hanauma (Courtesy of Francis Haar).

Petroglyphs existed at Hanauma, but have almost disappeared. Hawaiians sometimes carved petroglyphs at places of power, where they felt the mana was particularly intense.

Ancient Hawaiians sensed a concentration of spiritual power (*mana*) at Hanauma, and deemed it a tabu (*kapu*) place, meaning that only those of certain rank, such as kings and the nobility, or ali'i, were allowed within the protective arms of the bay. When they made an excursion, it was primarily for festivals and fishing trips. Both men's and women's hula competitions were held here, as well as uma wrestling tournaments. While these festivals were certainly exciting and entertaining, hula was also an important part of the ancient religion. These activities were considered sacred.

This tradition lasted almost as long as the monarchy. Although the kapu system was officially overthrown in the early 1800's, later kings still considered Hanauma their private fishing grounds even in the 1870's.

Ancient Hawaiians had poetic explanations for the creation of the bay. One legend tells the story of Keohinani, an extremely beautiful, kind, talented woman whose father was the guardian of Hanauma. Both Chief Koko and Chief Hana were in love with her. She appreciated both men equally. Not wanting to reject one by choosing the other, she called for an uma wrestling match between them. The winner would become her husband.

The chiefs were equally matched in skill and desire, and by evening, the score was tied. Keohinani could not choose between them, so she walked to the edge of the sea and asked her ancestral gods—her *akua* to turn her into the fair mountain behind the bay so that both suitors could gaze at her beauty eternally.

Pleased with this decision, her father asked to be turned into the hill encircling the bay, in order to guard both the bay and his daughter.

Another legend says that the form encircling the bay is a pair of *moʻo* (lizards). This is a form of guardian spirit for some Hawaiian families, but could be treacherous to others.

Despite, or perhaps because of the powerful tabus that kept most people away, Hanauma was known as a place where trysts occurred between forbidden lovers. The ancient society had strict laws forbidding certain relationships and the lovers who met here risked death if discovered.

Because Hanauma was used only for special occasions, some sacred and spectacular, others strictly tabu, it is imbued with an intense energy. At times, shimmers of this energy can be perceived—a momentary change of light, the chance scent of wet thatch, an echoed, whispering drumbeat, or the fleeting sensation of another presence—serving to remind us of those who fished and chanted, dreamed and danced, loved and laughed at this extraordinary place in times gone by.

Hanauma

is a natural learning environment where the children of Hawai'i and visitors from other lands can experience marine biology up close and in person. Hanauma's status as a marine reserve has allowed the bay to become a sanctuary for an abundance of reef fish. Because they are protected here, the fish aren't afraid of man, or his fishing lines and spear guns. Instead of swimming away the fish in Hanauma encircle human beings with curiosity and eagerness.

Besides being a window on marine life, Hanauma is also a good place to study geology and astronomy. The hill above the bay has been the site of star-path observation. From there one can see the Southern Cross, the rotation of the planets and most of the Milky Way. The arid climate assures a clear view most of the time. In fact, the University of Hawai'i sets up telescopes here for star-gazing sessions known as "star parties."

The birth of Hanauma can be dated to an undersea volcanic eruption about 35,000 years ago. (This is a much later period than the volcanic activity which created the rest of Oʻahu.) *Pele,* the Goddess of Fire, put on a magnificent display of her powers. As the lava was forced through the ocean floor, water rushed in the vents, causing the uprising magma to fragment. During the eruption, the vent shifted position, which created two overlapping craters. The fragmented lava hardened into tuff cones, similar to Koko crater.

The liquid fire spewed elements from the earth's mantle, mixing ash, silicate and basalt boulders together with limestone from the ocean floor. These form the structure of the bay. Olivine crystals give the beach its greenish color. These silicate crystals are what *haole* (foreign) visitors saw at Mount Leahi causing them to mistakenly call it Diamond Head.

An ancient tale recounts a spectacular battle between Pele, Goddess of fire and volcanoes, and *Namaka o kaha'i*, her older sister, who was a Goddess of the sea in their homeland of Kahiki. Pele made her powerful sister jealous over a man named Aukele and had to find a new homeland.

She came to Hawai'i, but her sister pursued her, filling in Pele's crater-homes with sea water. One of the supernatural forms Namaka o kaha'i could assume was that of stone. Part of Namaka o kaha'i was broken off in the battle she waged against Pele at Hanauma. This particular stone is said to glow faintly when provided with awa, a ceremonial narcotic drink.

Courtesy of The Volcano House

Once the fiery lava vent had moved along its course, other elements of nature went to work carving the tuff cones. Rain eroded gullies, wind swept away loose gravel, but it was the force of the sea that had the most dramatic effect. The strong current that begins far out at sea and ends by crashing against Hanauma's cliffs finally broke through the wall completely about 7,000 years ago. The ocean eventually filled in the crater and formed what is now Hanauma Bay. A similar effect can be seen off the coast of Maui at another marine reserve, Molokini Crater.

Today, the same strong currents still focus directly on the crescent edges— powerful waves barrage the corner of the bay at Pai'olo'olu Point (known affectionately as "the baboon's nose" or the "mo'o's head") in the area called the Witches Brew.

On a rough day, the tremendous impact of the waves against the cliffs launches the backwash up over 100 feet at times. One can see not only how the ocean broke through the wall of the crater, but how it sculpts the stone and is continually changing the shape of the bay.

These waves claim lives every year. Although many of the victims are visitors not familiar with the capricious powers of Hawaiian waters, accidents occur among locals who risk the surge zones looking for a shellfish delicacy known as 'opihi.

Thus, it is the 'opihi, not the shark, that Hawaiians referred to as "the fish of death." Despite the hazards of collecting it, 'opihi is and was very popular among Hawaiians. The volcano goddess, Pele, was also called "the goddess who ate 'opihi" and 'opihi shells were once used almost like money.

Because the 'opihi habitat is in the rough surge zone, they are famous for their stubborn grip on the rocks. Thus, the 'opihi is often used as a metaphor for stubborn or clinging types of people.

Even on a seemingly calm day, waves can rush unexpectedly over the ledge, taking unsuspecting people with them, often to their death.

*It pays to heed the saying
"Never turn your back on a Hawaiian wave"*

The area known as the Witches Brew got its name because it usually is a veritable cauldron, boiling furiously and filled with all kinds of strange ingredients, ranging from fishing nets to swimming fins. The currents flow in such a way as to make Hanauma, and the Witches Brew in particular, the final destination of nautical rubbish. This effect was most graphically seen when there was an oil spill in the channel between Oʻahu and Hawaiʻi. The oil came straight to Hanauma and collected at the southeast corner (known unofficially as 'garbage beach') and in the Witches Brew. This current has positive and negative sides. On the positive side, one can find occasional treasures among the rubbish, and certain types of large fish such as the *awaawa* like to hang out beneath the debris. It's more often the case that the debris is fatal to the marine creatures who live in Hanauma's protected waters. While Hanauma may be a refuge from spears and hooks, it is not protected from the pollution of military ships, oil tankers, commercial fishing operations and careless individuals who leave nets, toxic waste and rubbish in the ocean. In fact some of the fish at Hanauma are affected by "bento bacteria" from the way visitors dispose of picnic lunches. These factors will continue to pose a threat to the inhabitants of the bay until stricter regulations are enacted and enforced.

On the other side of the bay is Palea Point, an area known as "the Toilet Bowl." This lovely name is due to the way the ocean fills up the stone bowl with each surge only to have all the water flush out as the wave recedes. This works the same way as a blowhole, in that there is an undersea tunnel which is connected to a crevice farther in, a crevice that is home to a reef shark.

47

The Toilet Bowl is the lifeguard's nightmare. People jump in to ride the surge as it fills up and recedes, only to have a larger than normal set blast through—slamming heads into the rocks, or pulling people back down into the channel. It is a long walk back to help, and the lifeguards dread having to go into the dangerous crevice to fish out bodies.

49

Hawai'i's lifeguards are highly skilled watermen and women, monitoring as many as 10,000 people a day. The emphasis is wisely on prevention, and they are acutely attuned to the many variables in constantly changing conditions.

The keyholes are the absolute best places for swimmers to view fish.

Keyholes are the sand patches which are much deeper than the surrounding reef. *(Non-swimmers—beware—the drop-off is sudden.)* Fish flock to the keyholes to check out the dining possibilities.

For skilled skin and SCUBA divers, the best way beyond the reef is through the channel directly in front of the southernmost lifeguard tower. It is usually marked with a red flag. Trying to walk over the coral kills it and cuts one's feet as well. (However, there is very little beyond the reef that can't be viewed in the keyholes.) The channel was blasted by AT&T in 1957 in order to lay the first transpacific telephone cable. They also moved the boulders to the edge of the reef to reduce beach erosion, thereby enhancing the unique swimming conditions of the bay.

Rumor has it that an avid fisherman (back in the days before it was a marine reserve) used dynamite to blast the arch on the ledge out to the Toilet Bowl, Palea Point, so he could have an easy path to a favorite fishing spot. That was back in the days when people used to go and camp for weeks or months at a time. At almost any *kamaʻaina* gathering on Oʻahu, there will be people who can tell stories of camping there, often going by mule, and once in a while, by canoe.

During WW II, Hanauma was a military station, known as "Minnesota Beach."

Hanauma became a marine reserve in 1967, and a City and County Park in 1978. Since then, it's become one of the most popular attractions in the United States. There's an image in many people's minds that Hanauma is "how Hawaiʻi should be."

This feeling of déjà vu is not surprising. Many HAVE seen it before—in Elvis Presley movies.

Hanauma was the romantic location of Elvis' beach boy days in "Blue Hawaii." Several scenes were filmed here: Chad and Maile frolicking in the water and on the beach—his buddies magically appearing in a canoe, complete with guitar, ukulele and bongo drums! "Blue Hawaii" also featured a luau/hukilau shot at Hanauma complete with sand dancing.

In "Paradise, Hawaiian Style" Hanauma's Palea Point was the site of Elvis' helicopter crash.

(Photo courtesy of the DeSoto Brown Collection)

Hanauma

A rare native fern*

is not only a marine reserve but a reserve for plants as well. The Nature Conservancy has preserved over 30 acres in the crater above the bay, known as Ihi'ihilaukea, to protect a rare native fern. This fern is found in only two places in the world; this is one of them and is closed to the public, in order to protect the habitat.

The vegetation has changed in the last century—haole koa now occupies areas that once were full of native plants and grasses. Kiawe trees, bougainvillea and other foreign species are abundant, but there are still native plants surrounding Hanauma.

"Pōhuehue" or "morning glory" as it is more commonly known, grows in the sand. It was used medicinally by ancient Hawaiians, serving, among other purposes, as a protective, healing sheath after a circumcision. It was used for good magic, such as a surf-raising rite, and for the darker practices of sorcery. The Hawaiians, known for their metaphorical communication, would say that one was "smitten with the pōhuehue" if that person was a victim of sorcery. It was believed that one who bore ill against another would smite the sea with pōhuehue while the intended victim was at sea, and that this, along with the proper incantation, would cause the sea to become rough and dangerous, killing the victim.

A native flower is the delicate *'ilima*. It also was used for medicinal purposes, as is related in the saying: "Ola no i ka pua o ka 'ilima"— there is healing in the 'ilima blossom. 'Ilima is one of the first medicines given to babies as a mild laxative. It also makes a lei which was the favorite of royalty and today 'ilima is the symbolic flower of O'ahu.

(*Courtesy Marie Bruegmann)

'Ilima

Pōhuehue, beach morning glory

Naupaka

The *naupaka* shrub, with its half-flowers, commemorates the sad tale of lovers who are separated. One type of naupaka grows by the ocean's edge, and the other can be found in the mountains. One explanation of this is that young lovers were walking when they got into a senseless argument—the kind that happens often enough when we take someone for granted. One version says that the gods were disgusted with the way the young people were treating their love—a gift from the gods—and therefore separated them. Another version is that the man gave the woman a naupaka flower, back in the days when it was a full flower. The woman ripped the love offering in half, and the man died of a broken heart. Thereafter all naupakas grew in only the half-flower shape. Still another story says that the woman was angry, ripped the naupaka in half, and told her lover not to speak to her until he found another. The gods, upset by her reckless anger, turned all naupaka flowers into half-flowers, and so the young man died after searching in vain. The half-flower shape today is a reminder to lovers to temper their words and to think of their blessings of love before speaking harshly.

The leaves of the naupaka plant contain a chemical which helps keep diving masks from fogging.

REMEMBER—ALL THE PLANTS AT HANAUMA ARE PROTECTED

Hau

Paʻu o Hiʻika

A flower which is rare grows near the ʻilima at Hanauma. The small blue flower is known as *"Paʻu o Hiʻiaka"* or "Hiʻiaka's skirt." *Hiʻiaka* was the baby sister of Pele, the volcano goddess. One day Pele was searching for ʻopihi by the ocean's edge, so she put her sister far up on the rocks away from the surge. Hiʻiaka lay uncovered and her skin started to burn. A plant which had not been known to flower produced a blue blossom to cover the baby and protect her from the sun. Ever since, the flower has been known as "Paʻu o Hiʻiaka."

The *hau* tree is a type of hibiscus which grows well at the ocean's edge. The corky wood was used for canoe parts and fish floats. The sap was used in childbirth, to help make the birth canal slippery. Pregnant women began ingesting it in their seventh month for that purpose. The delicate hau blossom is considered symbolic of the transitory nature of the human spirit. Also, because the flower is beautiful but short-lived, there is the saying: *"Kiʻilili ka pua hau o kalena"* which refers to women who are good looking, but not good workers.

Niu-the coconut tree

When the wind whispers soft reminders of Hanauma's beauty, the message is usually borne on the dancing fronds of *niu* —the coconut. Hawaiians used this tree for everything. The coconuts provided water and food sources, the leaves were used for weaving. The trunk could be made into drums and the fiber used to make sennit or rope. In ancient days, the water of young coconuts (niuhiwa a kane) was used by priests in divination: "niu maka o noʻa ʻelaʻe—green coconuts for clear vision." "Wahi ka niu"—breaking open the coconut was a sign of piety. There are legends that speak of the coconut tree as being one of the forms that an eel can assume. Hawaiians also believed that if one dreamed of coconuts, it was a sign from the spirit that any project undertaken on the following day would meet with failure. In contrast, most of the people who frequent the bay today see the coconut tree as a symbol of romance, paradise, and adventure.

Hanauma's

undersea world is a galaxy of inter-related yet surprisingly diverse elements. Calcareous algae and coral are the main components of the reef. It takes nearly 100 years for the reef to grow just 10 inches—one of the reasons that taking or breaking the coral is strictly prohibited.

Each coral is actually made up of hundreds of living organisms which form a community—much like miniature nautical condos!

Once the coral is established as a foundation, *limu* (algae and seaweed) has a place to anchor. This brings the fish in to feed.

Staghorn coral

Coral is the foundation of the reef ecosystem

Walking on reef damages it

The ecosystem is very sensitive. Most of the inner reef at Hanauma is dead from people walking on it. The greatest destroyer of reef elsewhere on the island is building run-off, created when subdivisions are developed. In Hawaii some of the finest marine ecosystems anywhere in the world have been annihilated by irresponsible development. To a much lesser degree, coral is eaten by crown of thorns starfish and *uhu* (parrotfish) who eliminate it as sand—helping to create the beach.

There are many kinds of limu, although all but the most inaccessible are quickly eaten due to the large concentration of fish here. Limu is good for humans, too. Hawaiians use it as an integral part of their diets, recognizing it as a rich source of vitamins and minerals. Hawaiians called it "the fish that sways in the sea" or "long-haired fish" and someone whom they considered a drifter they called "he wahi limu pai"—seaweed washed ashore.

There are many kinds of limu native to Hawai'i

Crown of thorns seastar

Rose coral

Uhu eating algae

*Hermit crab**

It takes a close-up look at the reef for a myriad of other life-forms to become visible.

Sea cucumbers—*loli* to Hawaiians—have one of the more interesting defense mechanisms. They eject their entire stomach at an attacker. This charming creature was nevertheless harvested by the shipload and consumed with relish. It has an even more important function in the sorcery known as "Hana Aloha." Loli, in the hands of trained specialists, could make a powerful love potion.

*Sea slugs***

* *Courtesy of Art Reed.*
** *Courtesy of the University of Hawaii at Manoa Marine Option Program.*

Sea cucumber-loli

Flatworm*

Brittle star**

Anemones **

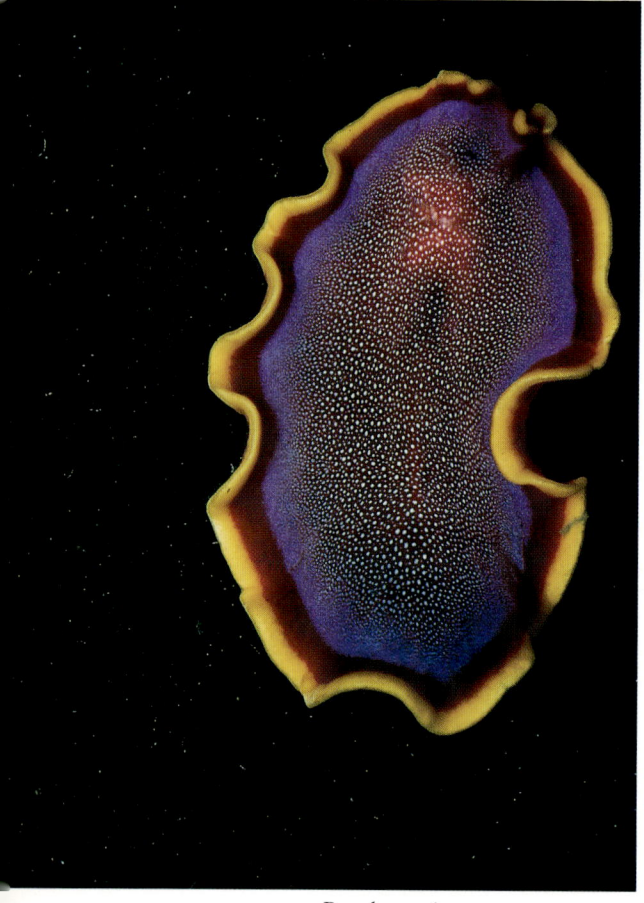

*Psuedoceros**

*Crab**

Spanish dancer eggs

*Courtesy of Art Reed.
**Courtesy of the University of Hawaii at Manoa Marine Option Program.

There are several types of sea urchins at Hanauma. The group as a whole were known as *ina* by Hawaiians and were referred to as "the fish that hurts the hands."

A demonstration of the Hawaiian harmony with the inter-relationships in nature is evident in the saying "When neneleaui blooms, the sea urchin is fat" and "When the urchin is fat, the parrotfish is good to eat."

The armor urchin "hā ʻuke ʻuke" lives in the rough surge zone.

Slate pencil urchins have a slight poison that leaves a red, itchy patch on the skin. The bleached spines were used by Hawaiians as jewlery.

The rock-boring urchin leaves trails in the reef as it tunnels in search of food.

This is the dreaded wana. The black spines release a very painful venom into the hand or foot that brushes against it. Vinegar or urine will help neutralize the toxin.

The collector urchin drapes bits of debris over itself, perhaps for camoflage.

Among the creatures in the crevice are the red nocturnal SQUIRRELFISH, 'ala'ihi (with stripes), King Kamehameha's favorite fish, and the Menpachi or 'u'u, which is a favorite eating fish today. Hawaiians referred to the 'ala'ihi as "the fish that pierces the hands" and it was a warning that someone was not to be trifled with if he was called an 'ala'ihi.

An eel, one of 30 types known locally

Squirrelfish (and boxfish)

In the same crevices where one finds squirrelfish, one can find the LOBSTER, referred to in slang as a "bug." This is an appropriate nickname not only because of the way lobsters look, but because they are the cockroaches of the sea. They scavenge everything they eat off the bottom of the ocean. It takes a lobster eight years to reach the legal weight for eating and it will squeak when caught. To avoid that fate, they usually live in very deep crevices, and are protected from man's hands by the resident eel which often presides over the lobster's home.

Lobster**

Far from being the vicious creature most people imagine, EELS, (*puhi* in Hawaiian) are generally shy. The menacing opening and closing of the mouth is just the eel's way of passing water over the gills. They usually only bite when something, such as a lobster-groping hand, invades their home. The bite is so dreaded not because it occurs frequently, but because once an eel does bite, it often doesn't release it's jaws. That means a chunk of the victim is often pulled out. Hawaiians called eels the "long fish of the sea," which were considered a delicacy. Of the roughly 30 types of eels known to ancient Hawaiians, legend has it that they feared only *puhi paka* which was known to devour everything in sight, and *puhi kapa*, a fierce eel that can go ashore in wet sand and was even seen climbing hala trees and dropping on people below. It couldn't move on dry sand. However, this eel is virtually unknown in modern times. *Puhi kina'u* was used as a medicine.

There are a variety of sayings involving the eel. "Love is like an eel, the creature that dwells in the sea cavern" meaning that love makes one restless in the mind like the writhing of an eel. To refer to someone as an eel was to call them hyperactive, but to call someone an eel with pointed teeth was a reference to their fierce fighting abilities.

The eel was often a warning symbol. "An eel of the sandbank is a dangerous creature" referred to a dangerous person. "Puhi okaoka" "an eel that chews into bits" was said of a Kahuna well versed in all branches of Kahuna practices—a person not to be trifled with. "The eel is a fish that moves skyward" refers to the coconut tree as one form of Niuloahiki, a deity who had the forms of eel, man and coconut. The expression is used to mean any influence that rises and becomes overwhelming—such as love. It also is used to warn of an ambitious person who will let nothing stand in his way.

** *Courtesy of the University of Hawai'i at Manoa Marine Option Program.*

He'e, tako, squid, devilfish—various names for the octopus

OCTOPUS are highly intelligent creatures. Their soft bodies allow them to slip into the smallest holes and they can change color to blend into the surrounding reef or to indicate a change of mood. Their best camouflage, however, is the ink cloud they disperse when threatened. The would-be attacker sees only the thick ink while the octopus slips safely away.

Octopus have a beak much like that of a parrot. While a bite can be painful, they are gentle creatures and can become quite friendly. The suction cups on the tentacles can make it a bit "sticky" to extract oneself. They have the ability to regenerate arms that have been bitten off.

Hawaiians call the octopus *he'e*. They considered it symbolic of the god-form in humans because it has no bones and can go virtually anywhere.

The octopus was and still is a favorite food among many people. The most common dish is to thinly slice a tenderized "squid," as they are sometimes called, and to marinate in spices to make "tako poke."

Hawaiians had a number of sayings relating to the octopus, ranging from regulations on the harvest: "Pua ko pua, ku ka he'e," which says that when the sugar cane tassels, octopus season is here (late October or November).

There were sayings which noted the octopus' intelligence such as "ku kae uli" which means "octopus ink." This label was attached to those who were clever at escaping precarious situations, primarily prostitutes during the whaling days.

There are quite a few more derogatory sayings. To tell someone that "yours is the mouth of an octopus" was to call the person a liar. "It is wonderful how the octopus notices the little cowries" was said sarcastically to a grown man who looked at young girls with lust. To tell someone they have the body of an octopus was to call them spineless, a weakling. And to say "It is a large octopus because it shows a red color" was a way of telling a man that he was sitting in such as way as to expose himself.

Octopus are highly intelligent.

The cowry is the octopus' favorite food.

Several types of fish come into the inner reef of Hanauma and can be seen inches from the shore. At certain times of the day *aholehole*, *manini* and even mullet or milkfish will form a tight group—a black cloud in ankle-deep water. More often these fish will just parade through in smaller bands, delighting visitors with their first glimpse of live fish in their own habitat.

Fish coming in to feed

MULLET were very significant to ancient Hawaiians. This was a fish of choice in most offerings to the gods, and often only the chief would be allowed to eat them. It was one of the principal fish in the elaborate fish pond system. The Hawaiians called them ‘*ama‘ama* or ‘*anae* depending on whether they were less than 12 inches or larger. This is now a way that men tease one another or brag about their "size"; "You're just one ‘ama‘ama." "No way, brah, I'm ‘anae!" The fish commonly migrate from Ewa Beach to Laie, and ones who have made the trek will have traces of red and darker scales. Mullet live in the warm in-shore waters, and perspire.

MOI are similar to mullet, but not as delicious, and therefore not as tabu. Moi are very active and it is said; "where the sea broils, dwells the moi." Someone who left home for a better chance of advancing but ended up coming back home was one who "returns to the broiling sea like a moi fish."

The NENUE is commonly seen inside the reef. Most are a grey color, but a few are yellow. The yellow ones are reputed to be the protectors of the school.

Moana

GOATFISH, so called because of the two whisker-like feelers extending from this species' chin, are among the very favorite eating fish today. Hanauma may be one of the few places one can see them for that reason. The *kumu* is the most highly prized. In the past, it was used as a primary offering in ceremonial sacrifices, especially for launching a canoe, for hula ceremonies and for the atonement for a "sin." It was also offered after one had completed a course of study, and could become a master or teacher, thus the Instructor in the halau is called the Kumu Hula. Women were forbidden to eat this fish, but apparently could use it as an offering. The young of the species (ahuluhulu) were used in a rite called "pa'ina ho'ok'u" which was a tribute of 'aumakua when the priest had delivered an afflicted person from death.

MOANA are friendly little fish that were said to have gotten their deep red color by eating *ohia lehua* blossoms. These fish love tidepools and will leap from pool to pool. The fish was used in "Hana Aloha" (love sorcery) to rid a person of an infatuation.

WEKE are also prized for eating, but eating the head can cause hallucination, delirium and nightmares.

Weke also were used ceremoniously for opening or releasing something, such as evil thoughts, or to open the door of a mystery to reveal the truth.

Weke

Kumu

Manini, friendly little fish that run in large schools.

Surgeonfish

SURGEONFISH are among the most common fish at Hanauma. Surgeonfish have a very sharp dorsal fin that can stand up. One variety, *manini,* referred to as "convict tangs" or "zebra tangs," are friendly little fish that stick together in large schools. There are various stages of development: *ohua-liko* (tender leaf bud), when they are the size of a postage stamp; *ohua-kaniʻo,* when the stripes appear (one day old); *ohua-haʻekaʻeka,* when they begin to eat seaweed; *kakala-manini* (half-grown) when they get the spine and finally full grown manini. This is a highly prized eating fish, and it was usually eaten whole. The small ohua-stages were often gathered, salted and dried on the rocks, to be popped into the mouth like snacks. Salting makes the dorsal fin lie flat. Eating a surgeonfish with a dorsal fin that wasn't entirely flattened was a hazard. It was said that if a pregnant woman craved manini, her child would be born affectionate, timid, and home-loving like the manini.

Manini were known as "the fish brought in

Yellow tang

Achilles tang

Palani

by the rain at sea," a reference to spawning. Millions of small manini are hatched during the summer months, and after a shower at sea, they will come to the shore, usually in the early morning.

Other surgeonfish one may see are *kole*, *palani*, *kala*, Achilles and yellow tangs.

PALANI are pretty, but have a strong odor. This odor is attributed to either of two legends. In the first, a young girl, Keʻemalu, was swimming far out at sea and needed help getting back in, so she called on her aumakua, which was the palani fish. He gave her a ride towards shore, but her desire to urinate became overwhelming, and finally she gave in, and covered the back of the palani. The other story goes that Punia killed a multitude of ghosts and rolled them up in a fish net and set them out to sea where they tainted the palani with their odor. Palani were tabu to men, but women were allowed to eat them. To say "it is a palani fish" was a rude remark about someone's body odor. And "the palani makes a strong smelling soup" was a warning that one with an unsavory reputation imparts his bad character to all he does.

KOLE are mild-mannered fish. Hawaiians traditionally put kole in the ground where the house posts were to stand facing the east. This was a protection from a kahuna entering the house and predicting trouble for the occupants. If the kole were there and the kahuna did this, he would die. If the kole

Kole

were not there, presumably his words would come true. Kole was a metaphor for stories, and so "It is interesting to fish for kole" is a way of saying it is fun to hear good stories.

KALA, unicorn fish, are also surgeonfish. There are several varieties of kala, but the one that looks like a unicorn was known as *kala lolo*—crazy kala. The sharp spike near the caudal fin is alluded to when one was called a kala—meaning "well equipped to defend one's self." These interesting fish can look almost human.

Unicorn fish, kala lolo (naso tang)

Milletseed/Common/Lemon Butterflies (Miliaris)

The BUTTERFLYFISH *(Chaetodon)* or what the Hawaiians called *kīkākapu* is one of the most abundant fish at Hanauma. The Hawaiian name means "energetic and prohibited." Butterflyfish are brightly colored and either friendly or hungry enough to follow divers and snorkelers around for hours at a time. There are many species—all yellow and black to some degree, and some can change their colors at night.

Racoon Butterflies (Chaetodon lunula)

Chaetodon trifasciatus

Chaetodon multicinctus

Teardrop Butterflyfish (Chaetodon unimacalatus)

Ornate butterflyfish (Chaetodon ornatissimus)

Lauwiliwilinukunukuoiʻoi

Lauwiliwilinukunukuoiʻoi (Forcipiger flavissimus) the longest named fish in the Hawaiian language, means "long-nosed leaf of the *wiliwili* tree." Or, it could mean "Long-nosed unpredictable fish." Hawaiians referred to someone who is confused as "gone with a fish called *lauwili*."

Related to the butterflyfish are ANGELFISH (*Centropyge potteri*). These fish have a very specific spawning period, usually the week before the full moon at dusk, when the lunar pull is most likely to carry the larvae out to sea, away from predators.

MOORISH IDOLS (*Zanclus canescens*) were called *kihi kihi* by Hawaiians.

TRUMPETFISH (*Aulostomidae*) are called *nunu* by Hawaiians. These fish are found cruising the reef, looking for fish to catch off guard. They are capable of expanding their mouths several times beyond its appearance and sucking prey in with force like a vacuum cleaner.

NEEDLEFISH (*Tylosauus crocodilus*) are sometimes out in the less crowded waters of Hanauma. These fish cruise close to the surface of the water.

HUMUHUMUNUKUNUKUAPUA'A
This famous fish is the subject of several popular songs in Hawai'i, and has been the official state fish of Hawai'i. It is a member of the triggerfish family. They are so named because their dorsal spine becomes locked in place when they hide in the reef and can't be released until the smaller spine is released like a trigger. Nuku-nuku-apua'a means "having a nose like a pig" and humuhumu means to fit pieces together—a reference to the triangular pattern. This fish is not good to eat and was only used by ancient Hawaiians to burn as fuel to cook better tasting fish.

Related to triggerfish are the FILE FISH— *o'ili* (squeaky sound or sudden appearance). These are rare, but occasionally wash up on the beach in great numbers. When this occurs, it is believed to prophesy the death of a great person. This phenomena was witnessed on O'ahu before the death of King Kalakaua. Despite the fact that he died abroad, the people of Hawai'i knew what had happened, due to the presence of these fish. It last occurred in 1985-1986, coincidentally (?) when Mary Kawena Pukui, one of the greatest resources of knowledge in and on Hawai'i, died.

Christmas wrasse

Halichoeres ornatissimus

WRASSES and PARROTFISH are quite common both inside the keyholes and at the outer reef. The fish are remarkable in that they are able to not only change color as they mature, but females of the species are able to transform into the opposite sex. This usually occurs when something happens to the male. The largest, most aggressive female will change into a male and resume his mating responsibilities—which can be considerable. Some wrasses spawn between 40 to 100 times a day.

Wrasses come in a variety of shapes and sizes. A single fish may have three distinctly different marking patterns and colors as it goes through the stages of maturity. One of the more interesting behaviors is demonstrated by the "cleaner wrasse." Each will set up a specific "cleaning station" and other fish of all types will line up to get the parasites cleaned and eaten off them. Often there will be three to four fish hovering nearby in the "waiting room" while a fish is being worked on.

Cleaner wrasse eating parasites from hīnālea (saddleback wrasse)

Hīnālea and *hilu* are the most common types of wrasse. They were kept on hand to be eaten as an antidote to the bitter awa that was consumed ceremonially. Hīnālea was used as an offering when a woman wanted to become pregnant.

Hinālea luahine

The HOU *(Thalassoma purpureum)* is said to snore like a human being when it sleeps in pools. In fact someone who snored would often be jokingly called "hou." A small, inoffensive person who will nevertheless fight when provoked was also called "hou."

Coris gaimard-known as the hilu

It was said that a woman who ate HILU when she was pregnant would have a quiet, attractive, well-behaved child. These people were called "a hilu belonging to a chief" because chiefs liked such people and often kept them in their courts. Some families worshipped the hilu as an aumakua, or a family guardian. There is a story of one such family:

One day long ago, the men of a village caught a large hilu in the net. It was cut up and distributed among the villagers. Those who worshipped the hilu did not partake of the flesh, however. It turned out that the hilu was Maʻiʻo, one of the two brothers who were the hilu gods. When Kaululena, the other brother, learned of Maʻiʻo's death, he changed himself into human form and walked through the village. He went from fire to fire and took the pieces of flesh, tossing them back into the sea. When he came to the house where those who worshipped the hilu lived, he overheard the man in prayer. After the man had finished, Kaululena addressed him. "Put lepa (tabu) flags around your house and gather all of your family into that space. A terrible punishment is coming to this land for those who ate the flesh of the hilu. I am the god whom you worship. The land will be flooded." And it was, except for the tabu area. Maʻiʻo came back to life, and the stripes he has today are from the cutting and fires.

Parrotfish and wrasse usually are intermingled with several types of other fish, and swim together in groups of two or three, unlike the surgeonfish, which usually hang out in schools. The uhu and wrasse have other things in common as well. For example the uhu or "parrotfish" changes sex like the wrasse. Parrotfish are able to form a mucous sac around themselves, and go to sleep for the night. Others will go into crevices or bury themselves in the sand. The uhu is also responsible for other transformations—its hard, beak-like mouth is built to bite off bits of coral, and it is uhu elimination which eventually forms much of the sand on the beach. The male uhu is the green colored fish and the female is the red. A rare black one is probably in the middle of a sex-change operation. Fishermen watched the behavior of parrotfish carefully while they were out on a trip, because it was an indicator of the behavior of the spouse at home. If the uhu were clowning around, the fisherman could be pretty sure his wife was fooling around, too.

This male uhu has undergone a sex change. At one point it was a female uhu (parrotfish).

The uhu was commonly used as a metaphor for a good looking person, and for a slippery person: "There is a desire for that uhu" was said when a choice person walked by. And "The uhu is attracted by the decoy" advised that if one wants to attract an attractive person, he must have something to interest him. "He will not be caught, for he is a parrotfish" referred to someone too wily to be captured.

Female uhu

Pufferfish

Nohu—the scorpionfish

The PUFFERFISH or balloonfish (*Tetradon tidae*) is a very docile creature with a wild trick. It can inflate itself like a balloon by swallowing air or water. Thus the Hawaiian name *'opu hue*, stomach like a gourd or *keke* meaning pot-bellied. They tend to act as guardians for squirrelfish. These fish have edible meat, but the organs and skin contain a highly poisonous nerve toxin, fatal to human beings. Hawaiians avoided eating it, especially if the fish had yellow teeth, which was an indicator of the toxin levels. Today the Japanese play a kind of Russian Roulette by eating *fugu* to display bravery. If the chef has properly prepared it, there is no danger, if he has not; instant death!

Another poisonous fish is the *nohu*—the dreaded SCORPIONFISH. It has a poison gland between the first and second dorsal spines, and since it likes to partially bury itself in the sand, people sometimes step on it. Legend has it that this fish is one of the "snorers" like the hou. Despite its poison, it was sought after for eating, but it was always cooked. The larger varieties tended to follow the man-eating sharks around, and some Hawaiians wondered if it wasn't the nohu that laid the eggs which hatched into sharks.

The porcupine fish is somewhat similar to pufferfish

Hawkfish are usually found resting on coralheads

SHARKS occasionally come into Hanauma, and there is one that frequents the Toilet Bowl area. Hawaiians called sharks *mano* except for the man-eating kinds which were known as *niuhi*. Hawaiians did not fear mano, and in fact, often fed and worshipped them as guardians in the sea (*'aumakua*). Usually each family or *ohana* had a chosen member known as a *kahu* who would feed and caress the shark. The shark, in return, would aid the kahu. There are numerous instances of a kahu being in trouble in deep water and the shark taking him safely to shore aboard his back. There are also stories of pet sharks driving man-eating sharks from the waters where people swam. *Ka'ahupahau*, the guardian shark of Pu'uloa, Pearl Harbor, is a well-known example of this.

Kahus and others who had shark 'aumakua avoided eating shark meat but most people enjoyed it (always cooked). No one, however, ate the meat of niuhi, the man-eating shark. This shark has eyes that glow at night. Only kings and specially chosen warriors were allowed to fish for niuhi—to do so without permission was an offense punishable by death. This was because it was believed that the one who captured the niuhi would acquire some of its powerful nature. In this same vein, when Kamehameha's mother was pregnant with him, she craved the eye of the niuhi. This was a sign that her child would be a fearless warrior. While the flesh was not eaten, the teeth were used for warclubs and domestic knives. Shark skins were used for drums. There is even a Hawai-

ing. He was executed. His warning remains as a reminder to be on one's guard.

There are many other sayings about sharks: "When the shark eats, he never troubles to look toward the foot of the cliff" said of a person who eats voraciously with no thought of those who provided it—one who shows no appreciation for what has been done for him.

"The chief is like a shark that travels on land." Chiefs had the power of life and death over people, and could kill on whim—as unpredictably as sharks. Similarly, a chief or a powerful warrior was referred to as "the niuhi shark that devours all on the island."

It was said that "when the wiliwili tree blooms, the shark bites." (The wiliwili tree blooms during the shark's mating season. This was also a reference to when a pretty woman blossomed, and the young men fought over her.)

"May I be eaten by Pele; may I be eaten by a shark." This oath was taken only very solemnly, the Hawaiians truly believing that if the sworn action was not fulfilled, he or she would actually be killed by fire or a shark.

"Where the sea is dark, sharks swim." Sharks are found in deep and muddy water.

And finally, a surprising but interesting correlation: "Shark is the fish, may love be persistent." Used in "Hana Aloha" sorcery (love potions).

If one sees a shark while swimming at Hanauma, the best thing to do is to swim calmly toward the shore and notify the lifeguard. There has never been a shark attack in the bay. Sharks, despite "Jaws" portrayals, rarely attack a strong creature. It is the erratic strokes of a sick or injured fish that usually draws the shark's attention. And like dogs or any other animal, they can sense fear and will take advantage of it. If you simply ignore the shark it will probably take a look at you, then continue on its way.

ian version of the Trojan horse in which the chief of Waikiki and some warriors hid in a shark skin that had been stretched over a frame, and delivered to the Chief of Ewa. As soon as they were inside the compound, they attacked.

There were people who were considered to be human forms of sharks. They always wore shoulder coverings to hide the shark mouth. An example of this is Nanaue. He lived on a farm on the way to the beach and would warn passersby: "Be careful lest you go head and tail into the shark." After they had gone, he would change into his shark form, swim to the sea from the river, and eat those he had warned. He was eventually discovered when someone removed his shoulder cover-

DAMSELFISH (*Pomacentridae*) were known as *kupipi*. Damselfish are very territorial because they attach their eggs to the reef and must protect them from being eaten.

ULUA, *omilu* and the juvenile form known as *papio* occasionally cruise Hanauma. These fish are terribly aggressive and have chased small sharks out of an area. When mature ulua are agitated, they turn black. The most unusual feature of this fish is its shape. It can be three to four feet long, two to three feet high and only a few inches thick. It's like swimming next to a door. These fish occasionally "ram" divers who linger too long in their territory, and have been known to intimidate people out of the water, although not at Hanauma.

"He cannot be caught, for he is an ulua fish of the deep ocean" was a reference to a fine warrior. "A fish of the deep who pulls the line taut" referred to the ulua and or to a fine lad. When a woman said she was "going to haul ulua" it meant she was going to find herself a strong man.

TURTLES used to nest at Hanauma, and several still live here, although they lay their eggs elsewhere. Turtles can live for over a century. They can stay on the bottom for up to two hours when they are sleeping, but usually surface every 10 minutes or so to breathe while they are swimming. Hawaiians called the turtle *honu* and considered it a symbol of the island (the word for land is *honua*). They have a saying "land is like a turtle, as it moves on" meaning that it passes slowly but inexorably from owner to heir. The turtles of Hawai'i are an endangered species so they must not be touched or harmed in any way. It's fortunate that there are still some around to appreciate.

Photo courtsey J. Watt / Pacific Stock.

HUMPBACK WHALES can sometimes be seen outside the mouth of the bay in the winter months, breeching and spouting, playing and sounding. Hawaiians called them *kohola* and *palaoa*, and thought of them as a representative of *Kanaloa*, the god of the sea. They were neither hunted nor eaten. Today, they are an endangered species. While

some countries ignorantly slaughter them, here it is illegal to come within 100 yards of them. Whales are the largest living creatures on this earth, and among the most intelligent and gentle. These mammals eat plankton in the north during the summer and spend their winters here playing, mating and giving birth. (Their gestation period is longer than humans.) Listen carefully from underwater and you may be able to hear them singing this year's song, which may last up to 30 minutes and changes annually. Other species such as pilot whales and even sperm whales cruise this coast.

Photo courtsey Roger Hess / Pacific Stock.

SPINNER DOLPHINS occasionally come into the bay to rest and play after feeding all night out at sea. Spinner dolphins can easily be recognized by their unique spinning and leaping acrobatics. Like all dolphins, they have a highly developed sonar system known to humans as echolocation. These marine mammals are extremely intelligent, social creatures, although they are much shyer around humans than other cetaceans. Perhaps they should be—Spinner dolphins are an endangered species. These mammals are often killed in improper purse seine operations and in driftnets. Hawaiians called them *naiʻa* and sometimes *iʻa lele* (leaping fish). It was forbidden to kill them, and to break the tabu could have meant instant death. Modern laws are a little less stiff. However, it IS a federal offense to kill, injure or harass turtles, dolphins and whales in any way, and that includes chasing them with a boat. (Dolphins sometimes enjoy playing in the waters off the bow of a boat, but altering course to follow them constitutes harassment.)

Hanauma is a marine reserve for all sea life, but all of Hawaiʻi is a marine reserve for turtles, dolphins and whales!